The Vultures are Circling

Poems

By Sharon Waller Knutson

Copyright© 2023 Sharon Waller Knutson
Photo by Albert Knutson
ISBN: 978-93-95224-72-7

First Edition: 2023
Rs. 200/-

Cyberwit.net
HIG 45 Kaushambi Kunj, Kalindipuram
Allahabad - 211011 (U.P.) India
http://www.cyberwit.net
Tel: +(91) 9415091004
E-mail: info@cyberwit.net

Printed at VCORE.

Acknowledgments

The following journals published these poems in one form or another:

Impspired: "Rehabbing Uncooperative Limbs" and "Mind Traveling."

Lothlorien Poetry Journal: "All My Sorrows Soon Forgotten," "Father's Day 2022," "July 16, 2022," "Mr. Crow." Temperatures in Triple Digits," "Tis the Season" and "Watching Over Ben."

Red Eft Review: "Saying Goodbye to Bobby."

The Five-Two: "It's the Husband."

Trouvaille Review: "On My 80th Birthday"

Verse-Virtual: "Ben's Dog," "He Thinks He is Mario Andretti," "Margaret and Me, "Naomi and Wynona," "The Vultures Are Circling," and "Why I Never Learn to Swim."

Writing in a Woman's Voice: "Dear Loretta."

Contents

Acceptance

Falling

On My 80ᵗʰ Birthday

Breakfast in bed:
a strawberry smoothie
stirred with Stevia
poured over ice.

Lunch in the kitchen:
spinach salad with slices
of chicken and cucumbers
dressed in olive oil.

Dinner in the dining room:
broiled lobster tails
baked potatoes and asparagus
drizzled with melted butter.

In the evening, we dance
cheek to cheek on the tile,
then walk up the hill
in the cool breeze.

How old do you feel and think?
a friend asks. My middle aged
mind answers fifty but Charley
Horse tells me it's closer to sixty.

The Vultures Are Circling

outside looking for dead meat
when inside I lose my balance
while putting away my fifteen-
pound dumbbells, slamming
my shoulder against the glass
hutch, then twirl like a tempest,

and bounce off the step
where I just did my aerobics
and land on my left shoulder,
arm and hip on the hardwood
floor, which feels like a pillow,
and holler for my husband
who is in the kitchen listening
to the screeching scavengers.

Feeling no pain, I sit up and try
to get to my feet but my eighty-
year-old joints are melded like
melted metal. The doorbell
ringer my mother-in-law used
to summon my husband when
she was dying at ninety-eight
sits on the nightstand, several
feet from my trigger finger.

I think of my eighty-seven-
year-old mother lying
in her closet with a broken

leg and her fingers drumming
on the linoleum until the tenant
below calls paramedics but she dies
anyway. I scream until it scares
away the buzzards and he finds
me in the corner crawling
on my hands and knees
towards safety and survival.

Everything Happens in Threes

my mother used to say:
births, deaths, accidents.
She is long gone when:
suffering from shingles,
in my sixties, I slip out of bed
and wander into the courtyard
where my husband is jamming

with musicians and back into a speaker
box which cuts me off at the knees,
bucking me backwards where my back,
buttocks and hip crash on the concrete
and my head is cradled by a craggy cowboy
sitting cross legged on the ground.

I see nothing but white and hear
voices coming from a tunnel.
She could have cracked her head
wide open. You saved her life.
I'm a nurse. Don't move, honey.
I remember someone carrying
me back to bed and feeling
bruised and sore for days.

Doing yoga at daybreak with Denise,
in my early seventies, I topple
over like a Saguaro landing
with a thud on the tile floor
while doing the tree pose

and brace myself with my left
hand, breaking the wrist and fingers.
In a cast for six weeks, my fingers
stay stiff and straight and my wrist
still aches in the cold or heat.

If mama were here, I would tell her
the third fall is not the worst
but I hope it will be the last.
I want to walk across the house,
the yard and grocery stores
without pain or fear of falling
until I fall asleep one night
smelling lilacs and lavender
and never wake up.

Legs

Long, lean and limber
as the dancers on the posters
in my grandfather's saloon,

they walked for miles on snowy
roads to school, on cobble
stone streets, dirt roads.

Waltzed with boys that came up
to my chin, two stepped, tangoed
with cowboys and college boys.

Ran up and down stairs.
Hiked up hills and mountains.
Jumped rope, kickboxed and bicycled.

First they stiffen and squawk
if I try to squat or sit in the tub.
I soak my swollen sausage feet

so I can get some sleep
before Charley Horse gallops
like a nightmare into the room

After the fall on the hardwood floor,
they fold like the chairs we sit on
at the potlucks and hootenannies.

Walking Through Fire

Barefoot I step into the stream
of tiny red ants swarming
across the bedroom tile,

smooshing and smashing
some, squishing others
between my toes

where they sting
like scalding hot water.
Aloe Vera gel soothes.

Blisters balloon and pop.
Soldiers retreat and regroup
until the next summer

when a battalion battles
under the bathroom
sink attacking bare feet

as I brush my teeth.
Shoes solve the problem
until temperatures soar

and a new troop tromps
and feet burst into flames
as I tap on the computer.

Only now there are no ants.
But the feet are still on fire.
Still scalding and screaming.

Zoom Poetry Reading

You are welcome to join us,
the email invitation reads
from South Carolina.
You are our first guest.
You could read a poem
from your new book.

I tell her my voice
is as weak as my legs
and ask if she would read
my poem and if my book
gets here in time I'll hold
it up to the camera.

She agrees and my husband
says he'll set it all up
and I can lie in bed
and watch it on the big screen
TV hooked up to my laptop.

The day of the reading, I rise
early, shower and shampoo
and take pain medication
and close my eyes in bed.
When I open them again,
I realize I have slept
through my first poetry reading.

The emails have piled up
in my inbox like vehicles
on the freeway in a rainstorm.
Where are you? We are waiting.
Hope it's the time zone fiasco.
in Phoenix and you're alive.

Why didn't you wake me?
I ask my husband as he walks
in the room. *I'm sorry the soup*
got cold. You were sleeping
so soundly I didn't want to disturb you,
he says scooping up the bowl.

Never mind the soup. I slept through
my own poetry reading, I say
sitting up in bed. *Was that today?*
he asks. *The book didn't come*
either. My friend emails: *No Problem.*
The group loved your poem.
You can meet them next month.
I stretch out my legs on the heating
pad and zonk out on another pain pill.

He Thinks He is Mario Andretti

because he has had lots of practice
wheeling his parents around
before they succumbed to old age.
Like them, I am an unwilling passenger.
Keep your feet up, he says.

I try maneuvering the wheelchair
around on doctor's orders.
It'll build up your shoulders and arms
so you won't have to lift weights.
But our house is like an obstacle course
and steering the wobbly wheelchair
was harder than it looked, and I fear
bumping my injured knees.

With my husband steering the ship,
we speed past the dining room table
he made with cactus wood
and pine with his own two hands.
The couch and loveseat we purchased
at the small furniture store
on Apache Trail in the junction
as soon as he put the doors
on the home he built out of clay
with the assistance of a carpenter
who carried the logs on his shoulders
and hoisted them to the ceiling.

Hold in your elbows, he commands
as we fly through the tight threshold
to the master bedroom – bigger
than some apartments – making a sharp turn
and through another threshold
to the master bath
where the jetted tub sits empty.
Wish I could take a soak, I say.
Maybe I could rent a forklift
to deposit you inside, he says
with a straight face. I do not laugh.
Bring me the walker, I say.

Don't Tell the Kids, He Warns Me

But I don't like to lie so when
our daughter calls, I blurt out
I fell and I am on a walker.
She teases me. *You didn't have*
to fall to try out grandma's
walker. Her laughter has a hint
of hysteria, a gene inherited
from her father to hide
the sensitive side inside.
Her brothers got it too,
but although they laugh
like hyenas in the wild,
they are herd animals.

And I know she is texting,
and Facebook messaging
as soon as we hang up, *Mom/*
Grandma is in trouble,
and like bellowing buffalo
her brothers and the grandkids
will hop in their trucks
and will be stampeding,
their hoofs hollow on the highway
heading for Arizona
where they buried a brother
and uncle just a year ago.
Don't come, my husband texts.
Everything is under control.
They skid to a stop and turn around.

Funny how Fallin' Feels Like Flyin'

Jeff Bridges croons from the television
playing Bad Blake, the drunk country
star singing in a backwoods saloon
as I lie in bed watching *Crazy Heart*
for the umpteenth time, but this time
the lyrics have a new meaning
other than falling in love with my favorite
actor over and over again.

Falling did feel like flying, I think
as I take one step at a time
gripping the handles
on the walker, fully aware
that at any time I could fly
over the bars like on a bicycle
or soar sideways or backwards
and land on my back like the sparrows
seeing blue sky as they fly straight
into our windows and conk their heads.

Some lie still until they stiffen
and predators snatch them off
the sidewalk. But others sit up slowly
like the nurse tells me and then fly away.
I hope I am able to soar in blue sky
a little longer like my idol Jeff
whose lymphoma is in remission.

Naomi and Wynona

Her big henna hair piled high,
mama rocks in her chair
as the redheaded mother
and daughter rock the stage
of the Grand Ole Opry.

Grandpa tell me about
the good ole days, the duo
harmonizes as Mama sings
along and daddy looking
like the Oak Ridge Boys
with long white hair
and beard reclines in a vinyl
La-Z-Boy the same material
as Naomi's red dress.

Wearing black like Wynona,
I sing off key as they harmonize:
You been lookin' for love
all around the world.
Baby, don't you know
that this country girl's still free?
Why not me? Why not me?

Daddy's been gone a year
and mama lies in the hospital
bed in the living room
every bone in her back broken
from Melanoma, while Naomi
in remission from Hepatitis C

prances around the stage in red,
blue and gold gowns
and Wynona dressed in black
cured of laryngitis growls, *Grandpa,*
tell me about the good old days,
at their televised farewell tour.

Mama lies beside daddy in the cemetery
while I sit up in bed watching the news
a month after my eightieth birthday
and two weeks after my fall
when Naomi's daughters announce:
We lost our beautiful mother to mental
illness as she lies in the morgue.

I hobble on my walker, then eat
dinner as the camera catches
Wynona boarding her bus
for the tour without her mother.
She would want this, she says.
I change the channel to watch
Wynona's sister, a mirror image
of her mother tell Dianne Sawyer:
Suicide. A firearm was involved.

Mickey and Me

I overlooked an orchid while searching for a rose.
The orchid that I overlooked was you, Mickey Gilly
in sleek dark hair and sideburns sings from the stage
to me in the seventies, both in our thirties,
as newly divorced I watch him on television.

Well, I spent a lifetime looking for you.
Single bars and good time lovers were never true.
I was looking for love in all the wrong places,
Mickey sings to me from the movie screen
as John Travolta and Debra Winger two step
and ride the mechanical bulls in his honky tonk
in 1980. I am forty and he is forty-six.

Mickey Gilly passed peacefully at eighty-six,
his widow announces on Instagram
after I turn eighty and my soul mate
sings: *Now that I've found a friend and a lover;*
I bless the day that I discovered
You, oh you; at the local cafe the same day
Mickey is buried by his family.

Recovering

Recuperating in a Wildlife Habitat

In the darkness, the wings
of a moth flutter against
my lips as I sip tea and startled
I drop the cup, a river running
by the bed. I turn on the light
and a grasshopper squats
and spits tobacco on the greens
on last night's dinner plate.
At daybreak, a crippled coyote
cries and limps, licking
his sore paw before quenching
his thirst at the waterfalls
in the front yard. Afternoon,
in the courtyard, a cheeky
chipmunk and a bushy tailed
squirrel duke it out on tippy toes
as I lie in bed feet propped
on pillows watching through glass.

Rehabbing Uncooperative Limbs

Your road is too rough,
says the physical therapist
and sends me a video
of a macho man who looks
like he could bench press
the brahma bull bellowing
outside my window. Surprisingly
I can squat and extend my leg
from my knee until it screams
and I realize I am not exactly
an athlete with a sports injury.

I google strengthening leg
exercises for seniors
and click on a video of a male
millennium with hair on his chin,
a belly that never birthed a baby
and calves that never squealed
like they were being lassoed
by a cowboy on a stallion.

When he twists his body
into a pretzel, I turn it off
and drag out my Denise Austin
tapes and pop them in the VCR.
She in a red leotard - mine doesn't
fit me anymore - and me in elastic
Bermuda shorts and a baggy shirt,
stretch and squat and cha cha cha

until I lose my breath and sprawl
on my back on the bed and bicycle,
hang onto the bedpost in tree pose
and play like a plank of wood on the bed.

My legs are grumbling and groaning
as I graduate to Gilad's workouts
with weights and aerobics.
High on endorphins and adrenalin,
I add weight and minutes to my workout
and feeling strong and invincible
I step, strut and soar on legs stiff
and shaky until they collapse
like a house made of matchsticks.

After the Relapse

I am brushing my haystack hair,
dismantling the rats nest,
matted and knotted
from drowning in a sea of sleep.

Once clear and cool as the wavy
water weaving through the canyon,
my mind is muddy and murky
as the meandering creek beds.

Showering and shampooing
in my uphill battle to walk
through the blazing forest
fire in my feet, knees and legs.

My breath, energy in short supply,
I emerge clean, sweet scented
and pure as the lilacs and lilies,
happy to be home in my own bed.

The Old Ladies Club

We all meet in urgent care.
Harriet who wears a hairnet
over her salt and pepper hair coiled
in a bun like a king snake
is having her blood pressure checked.
My husband is getting an epi pen
after being attacked by hornets.
Graying Gertrude is getting
a shot so she doesn't get shingles.

White haired Martha with dark
spots all over her arms and face
is a hypochondriac, Gertrude
tells me while Martha sees
the doctor. *Whatever we get,*
she gets. Harriet invites me
to join the Old Ladies Club.
We meet at 2 pm Wednesday
in each other's houses.

What do you do at this club?
I ask. *I knit*, Harriet says. *I quilt.*
Gertrude says. *I crochet*, Martha
says. *We gab about grandchildren.*
What do you do? They all groan
when I say, *I write poetry.*
You aren't going to bore us with:
I bought a lime for a dime.

Is that a crime? recites Gertrude.
We all laugh. *Count me in, I say.*

As soon as I walk in, the ladies start
pulling pill bottles out of purses
and lining them up on the counter.
Harriet hands over Lipitor,
Prilosec and fentanyl.
.
Gertrude lines up Haldol, Ativan and morphine.
Martha forks over Lithium and Zoloft.
What's your pleasure? Martha asks me.,
I feign an allergy attack and run to my car.
I am not going from the Old Ladies Club
to Arizona State Prison with the crafty three.
.
As we approach Urgent Care, I am on
alert for Gertrude's Grand Am, Harriet's
Cadillac and Martha's Mazda
and as soon as I spot all three
pulling into the parking lot
I slouch down and direct my husband to drive
to the next Urgent Care down the road.

Mind Traveling

In a wheelchair with Novocain numb feet,
knees stabbed by knitting needles
and starched stiff legs, I imagine I am:

In the Bay Area with Abha walking
along the embarcadero, Third Street
Bridge to Mission Bay Kids Park
where we watch the wind whooshing
under the wings of her granddaughter
as she flies on a swing like a swallow.

In Santa Monica Mountains with Rosie
hiking three miles in Corral Canyon Park,
seeking shade under alders and willows,
brushing away tall grasses opening
and shutting like saloon doors.
Eating fish and chips at the Malibu
Shrimp Shack satiated and satisfied.

In Pennsylvania with Margaret
sipping lemonade on the patio
of the five-bedroom house
where she has lived for fifty years,
the last sixteen years alone
as a widow and empty nester.
Reminiscing about interviewing
JFK, she in Dover and me in Billings.
two underage Jackie Kennedy look alikes
about to be baptized in a blood bath in Dallas.

In, Maryland with Marianne and Ethan
where their cat Thelma watches
a crow from the windowsill as we walk
to the Plaza Oaxaca and eat shrimp tacos
beneath the locust trees. board a bus
to Rock Creek Park, listen to the singalong
as colorful cardinals, finch, thrush, sparrows
perch on ash trees, follow the path to DC
where Sonny Rollins plays at the Hamilton
and Danilo Perez stops by. After sax
blaring and piano rocking in a jazz jam,
we somersault to the subway.

In New Jersey walking in the woods
with Michael and Laurie
as swarms of starlings swim
in the sky like swirling smoke
then swoop above our heads
like a scene out of the sixties
Hitchcock movie. We gape, gawk,
duck and dizzily dance at dusk
but these black birds don't attack,
just murmur and mesmerize.

In Vermont with Kelly and Mark
walking their white Korean Jindo
along a trail where a fox flits,
intoxicated by lilac perfume
as we watch a rabbit stalked
by a hungry hawk dive
under the back deck.

Young No More

You don't look a day over eighteen,
the twenty-five-year-old sailor says
as I try to convince him to take me
to a San Diego club on my thirtieth
birthday. *I have ID,* I say, flashing
my driver's license and tucking
it in my jean's pocket before he
can inspect it and realize I am older
than him and dump me for a bimbo
begging the bouncer to get in.

You're about twenty-eight, the guys
say when I turn thirty-six in Mexico
and forty-two in Idaho. I nod and smile.
I don't admit my real age until I am
seventy-nine. *If you're almost eighty,*
I want some of that Arizona water.
the hospice nurse says as she cares
for my mother-in-law in Idaho

You're an ageless beauty, my husband
says but as I brush my teeth.
I feel like the old crow cawing
in the courtyard until I color my brown
spots beige, pencil in eyebrows
and cover my naked lips Revlon red.

Playing Gin Rummy in Invalid Land

The ceiling fans are galloping
to cool down triple digit temperatures
and jets are roaring overhead
on their way to quash the latest blaze
in Tonto National Forest,
bordering our boundaries.

He is slumped in a folding chair
in his boxer shorts and t-shirt
and I'm in my nightgown
with the ripped sleeve sitting
on the edge of the bed, fanning
myself with my cards when I see
a six in diamonds to match
my five and seven and pick it up.

Put that back, he says, *You just drew
a card.* Normally, he'd let it slide,
since the accident, but instead
he reaches across the TV tray
and snatches the card, his elbow
knocking the red cup full of coke
crashing to the floor. I lift my feet
as the sticky brown liquid pools.
+
You don't care about me, he says
on his hands and knees soaking
up coke with a Kleenex. *I nearly
fainted and fell off the roof*

and then got calluses on my feet
running all over Wal-Mart looking
for your cursed cherry pie and crackers
they don't even carry.

I run my fingers through his white mop
of hair and promise to concentrate and
we continue the game until I tie the score.
Instead of checking to make sure
my cards all match, he folds
up the deck, tray and chair and doles
out the Benadryl and Tylenol for both
of us, brings me my cherry pie and flops
in bed beside me snoring like a bear.

I take it you didn't summon me for sex

my husband says with a smirk
standing in the doorway with the wheelchair
as he sees me sitting on the bed naked.
I smell like a sewer, I say. *I need a shower.*

He scoots me in the chair and hands
me the shower cap and body wash
and helps me to stand and hold onto
the bar with one hand and soap
and suds with the other. I whirl
around and step on the left foot
and a sharp pain stabs and stings.

I stepped on a nail, I shout through
the curtain. *There are no nails,*
he says. By the time he turns
off the water and helps me back
in the wheelchair, my foot feels
like I am stepping on a bed of needles.
He checks my foot. *No nail. No needles.*

He helps me towel off and slip back
into my nightgown and the nerves
play a symphony.as the cool air
from the ceiling fans hit my skin.
The sheet feels like sandpaper.
I grit my teeth until lunch
when I can zonk out on Tylenol
and get some relief like an addict
going from one shot to another.

Welcome to My World

With a Scorpion bite you
only feel excruciating pain
for three hours, a friend once said.
My left foot has been throbbing
and swollen for six hours. I tell
my husband to bring me an aloe
vera leaf from the plant in the patio.

I think I've been bitten by a scorpion,
I say. *I searched the shower and there*
were no scorpions or spiders sliding
in or out of the drain, he says.
He hands me the leaf and I spread
the gel on my sore foot. It soothes
and soon the soreness goes away.

The next morning I sprint on limber
limbs and healed foot to the computer
and the bathroom and even the kitchen.
I've been cured, I tell my husband,
By an imaginary needle, nail or scorpion.
He smiles and smirks as he heads
to the mailbox to check the mail.

He returns with a white plastic bottle
with a label ribboned in red, white
slate with black letters announcing:
Healthy Feet & Nerves, opens the cap,
and hands me a capsule. *Read*

The instructions, I say. *Take two capsules*
twice a day. If pregnant or nursing
consult a health practitioner before use,
he says as he disappears through the door.

The capsules are swimming in water
down my pipe as I laugh and stick
in the valley between my breasts.
I grab a handful of crackers
and wash them down with water
as my knee protests and I lay
my leg down on a heating pad.

My cell phone blares: *Welcome*
to my world, as Elvis in tight
white pants and shirt embroidered
with flowers, and a red scarf
around his neck sings and swivels
his hips and I am transported
to Hawaii like I was in the sixties
removing the scarf from his neck
singing along with him.

Welcome to my world
Won't you come on in?
Miracles, I guess Still
happen now and then.
And I believe and l am baptized
in holy water and I will walk
all over the world again.

All My Sorrows Soon Forgotten

The clock says 7 am and the sky
is gray and I am not sure if
it is morning or night until I see
my breakfast smoothie on the tray.
It looks like it is going to rain, I say.
*I hope not. The last of my roofing material
just came in from Lowes*, my husband
says as he jumps in the pickup truck.

In my inbox is an email from my cousin,
the brother I never had, the same size
as me when he was two and I was one.
His mother dressed us in identical
shorts, shoes, and socks and pushed
the double stroller all over Columbus.
Aren't my twins adorable? she'd gush.

I tried calling but your line was busy,
he writes, now at 81. *I lost my youngest
son on Memorial Day. Aneurism.*
I remember Shane, the same age
as Ben, both of our sons now dead.
I was supposed to go first, he writes.
The same thing I said when I called
him a year ago to tell him about Ben.

Lightning sizzles, thunder roars
like a jet taking off on the runway,
cows huddle under the ironwoods

and water drips and drizzles
then pours and floods the courtyard
as I wobble to the window to watch
while my husband loads shingles
on the truck bed in Mesa.

And my cousin in Billings makes plans
for a military service with his son's
marine buddies in the fall and to cast
his son's ashes in July on a hill between
Island Lake and Mystic Lake
where they hiked and caught rainbow trout.
My other son's dog Buddy is there.
That's where I want to be too, he says.

Flash Flood

My cell phone shrieks an alarm
that startles and chills my spine
just as thunder claps following lightning
pirouetting and curtsying in the window.
A female voice warns of a flash flood,
to stay inside, as if I had anywhere else
to go. The internet and power disappear.
We open the drapes and watch as water
pours down in sheets, flooding the yard,
the courtyard, the driveway and the washes
forming a network of streams and lakes.

We eat tuna fish sandwiches and watch
the two hour long fireworks and water show.
Suddenly, the sun shines and the show is over.
The internet and power are back and we
catch up on emails and resume our video.
The trees green up as they drink their fill.
The next morning my husband heads
for town to pick up supplies and groceries.
I picture the sky opening up and water
turning freeways into rivers and his Ford
truck floating out to sea with him steering
the ship to keep it oncourse. He returns truck
wheels muddy from driving the dirt road,
splashing through water in the wash
but he and his bounty are dry as a bone.

Independence Day

After ten hours sleep,
I awaken full of energy
and with a positive attitude.
Since I did Tai Chi, Yoga
and weights yesterday,
I write a new poem,
revise two others, cut
and paste them in my book.

My scalp itches, my back
groans and my legs stiffen.
I ring the bell, but he doesn't
appear. He is either on the roof
repairing leaks from yesterday's
monsoon storm or he is the office
wearing earphones as he listens
to and sings along with George Strait
as he sings Amarillo by Morning.

I turn on the shower water, slip
out of my nightgown, suds
with body wash, shampoo
my hair and feel the hot water
soothing sore spots and washing
away the dirt, soap and sorrows.

As I yank back the curtain
I hope to see his steady shape
standing there smiling holding

a bath towel but there is no one
there so I gingerly step
from mat to mat, grab a towel
off a rack and dry my body
and hair for the first time since
the fall. I put on my purple
pullover and Bermuda shorts
and with my comb smooth out
the tangles in my hair and life.

Milestones

Mother's Day

May 9, 2021

Happy Mother's Day he shouts
to his grandmother and me
from the submarine as sailors
laugh and cheer
in the background. His voice
is jubilant. *I'll be retiring*
from the Navy after twenty years
in twenty-four days. A cork pops.
and the sailors cheer. *Tell dad to meet me*
at the Phoenix airport June 4.

I've scheduled job interviews
for two weeks. When he visits
in February for six weeks using his leftover
leave, he talks about living in the RV
behind our house and commuting.
Happy to have his feet on solid ground
and not a moving ship he walks his hound
and climbs the Elephant Rock daily.
Can't wait to live out here for good.

After he hangs up. we gather Mother's
Day cards from the mailbox on the road.
for his 97-year-old grandmother
and I read mine in my inbox.
Instead of picking him up at the airport,

we pick up his sons and his ashes
and a month later we put red roses
on the grave of his grandmother.

May 7, 2022

The phone is silent. The flicker sings
and tap dances on wood. The cows mosey
in for chow and water and the bucks
and does square dance around the pond.

My husband returns from the mailbox.
No Mother's Day card from her or him.
Starts to pick up the phone and remembers.
Puts it back down and turns on his computer.
Returns from a hike with a bouquet
of yellow, orange and blue wildflowers.
I put them in a vase full of water.
hoping to keep them alive as long as I can.

May 25, 2022

The phone rings and I hear
that same soothing voice
coming from the Navy
officer as a year ago,
when he says: *I am sorry to inform*
you your son passed away today.

We stare at him in disbelief, thinking:
No. No. No. You've got the wrong
house, the wrong family. Not our son.

But a year later he is saying,
The first anniversary is hard
so if you need anything
just call and leaves his number
on the answering machine.

I get our son's Navy hat
and the flag the sailors folded
into a V shape at the twenty
one gun salute and flag
ceremony and put them
on the table and remove
all his pictures from the wall
and set them in a circle
like the family sat at the ceremony.

I feel hysteria creeping over me
as I can't find the only photo I have

of him peering around a corner,
his eyes smiling, his lips teasing
telling us he is up to something.

.

I rummage through all the drawers
until I find the photo I put away
when I came home after caregiving
to find the red and white roses
on his memorial wreath dead
and him looking so alive
in the black and white photo

smiling as he stares at me
and screamed and screamed,
drowning in guilt and shame.
How could I have let him go
that day. If he hadn't left.
he'd be sitting at the table today,
not his stupid hat and photographs.

I love you, both, I hear him say.
You couldn't have known.
And I light a candle and his father
and I remember him sitting on
the couch with his hound, Sol
and saying, *This is one of the best
days of my life* as he smiles.
My husband shows me the photo
on his phone and we say: *This
is going to be a good day.*

Ben's Dog

Feb. 2021

His name is Sol, our son says
as he enters our Arizona home
with the dog on a short leash,
but I hear *Salt* because he is white
and pure as the substance scattered
in the sea where they live in Virginia.

A rescue. Some kind of hound,
Ben says. I see white lab head
and sleek spotted greyhound body
as he sprints across the tile floor
and lands in my lap, licking my face,
and English Pointer in the photo.

His left leg lifts, tail stiffens
and nose points like a finger
at a covey of quail landing
on the rocks of our waterfalls
while he stands silent by the side
of our sailor son collared and leashed.

I can't let him off the lead or he will take off,
our son says as Sol strains and sniffs
the trail where they take their daily
hike up the rocky butte he climbed
as a kid. Sol sits patiently as Ben
plucks the Cholla needles out of his paws.

The only time Sol barks is when Ben
steals his rubber duck. From the windowsill
the dog silently stares at the mule deer
drinking at the pond and bolts
like the deer as our hand reaches
for the camera or he hears a loud bang.

As he whimpers, our son cradles his hound
like he did his babies. Sol follows Ben
from room to room and runs from door
to door when he goes grocery shopping.
Sol is still watching at the window for Ben,
says his girlfriend a year after his death.

Watching Over Ben

At midnight I rise from my bed
and wander on weak wobbly legs
to the kitchen for a slice of cherry
pie with a scoop of vanilla ice cream
wishing he was here to share it.

Rain slants down in sheets,
thunder roars like the cougars
and I look for him as lightning flashes
on the rock mountain shaped
like an Elephant, wanting to take
him a raincoat, an umbrella,
a dry change of clothes, a cup
of coffee and a cinnamon roll.

But my legs are even less reliable
than they were that humid July
day when one son took one arm
and the other the other arm
and helped me up the slope
to the mountain where I sat
on a rock while they carried
him to the top and left him there.

I know his spirit shed his skin
like the snakes and lizards
and he has no need for food
or water but still I want to take
him a bean burrito and watch

his blue eyes sparkle as the cheese
and refried beans drip down
his chin and through his fingers
like the last time we shared a meal.

Talking to a Friendly Voice

I'll call you today. I have something
important to tell you, my friend emails.
My husband brings me the landline
receiver before he goes up on the roof.

When it rings right away, I pick it up
confident it is my girlfriend, a relative
or a driver delivering roofing material.
A male voice asks for me by name.

It is familiar but I can't recognize it
until he says with that familiar laugh:
I'm glad you answered. You're the first
person I could reach today and I am tall.

I know exactly who is on the line
even before he says. *This is Joel*
from the police association,
and I hang up before he convinces

me to write a big fat check
when I never donate money over the phone
like he did a couple of years ago.
But then he had said in a flirtatious tone:

I am so glad you answered. I thought
I would have to get out my answering
machine. I didn't even know he wasn't
who he pretended to be until I heard his voice

months later in Idaho calling my mother-in-law
by her first name and spouting the same
seductive spiel and I screamed at him
like I did my cheating ex-husband.

But of course, he didn't hear the betrayal
in my voice because he just kept talking
in his aw shucks country voice
and I realized I was romanced by a robot.

Joel did not exist. But in Arizona
lying on the bed with no one to talk to
I wish he would call back, but he doesn't.
I dial my Jersey friend and get a busy signal.
Were you talking to Joel? I ask
when she finally calls. *You mean*
that funny guy from the police
association. How did you know?

Temperatures in Triple Digits

The big black brahma blares his horn
to protest sore feet from dragging tons
of muscle and flesh across the desert.
He preaches and prays for rain.

The javelina sprawl in the sand and spa
like chemo patients in pain. Too hot to holler.
the coyote pack trail their tongues and tails
past the mesquite, cholla and saguaro.

With sweat staining their hide,
the does and bucks circle the water,
waiting their turn. The hammering ceases
as the flicker and my husband take a siesta.

I lie on cool sheets behind clay
walls, sipping lemonade and tea
over cubes of ice and reading Steinbeck
and drifting into delightful dreams

where I walk up and down the grassy
hills of my childhood in Montana,
the cobble streets of Mexico and take
the trolley through Toronto.

Father's Day 2022

Static crackles on the landline
like crumpled up aluminum foil.
Is that you Ben? I whisper
picturing him calling on his cell
phone from whatever dimension
he is traveling through these days.
I pick up the wooden walking stick
my husband whittled from a Palo
Verde and hobble down the driveway,
holding onto my husband's arm
as the hot air propels us to the road.
Feeling feet numbing, legs aching,
I start to head back to the house
when a balloon floats above, snagging
on a barrel cactus across the road.
He runs to retrieve the blue balloon
with black letters shouting
Happy Father's Day, desperately
blowing air into the flattened balloon
like he is giving CPR to a hiker
we find collapsed on the road.

July 16, 2022

In a gown made of silk, satin and lace,
layered like her wedding cake,
our redheaded granddaughter
stands on her deck decorated
with purple and pink wildflowers
and western memorabilia. Wearing
black cowboy hats and boots,
matching tuxedos, camo vests
and orange ties her six-year-old son
and groom flank her on either side
as the sun slants through the Bing
Cherry Tree, Elephant Hart Plum Tree
and Dwarf Honey Crisp Apple Tree
in the suburb of Salt Lake City.
As she says her vows and tosses
her bouquet, we watch on our cellphone
from the Arizona desert, just a year
after sun sifted through the Idaho
pines as we placed white and red roses
on the grave of her great grandmother.

First Outing Since the Fall on the Floor

We exit Superstition Freeway
at Idaho Road, cruise past
Countryside RV Resort,
where two decades ago we rode
golf carts past palm trees
to collect rents at park models,
now replaced with new models
from new generations of snow
birds that fly in for the winter.

Turn left on Apache Trail,
right on Highway 67. left
into the parking lot, past
the Barber Shop where my husband
got haircuts while I bought
cookie jars and salt and pepper
shakers from the Antique Mall
and organic produce, vitamins
and herbs at the Good Apple
Natural Market on Plaza Place.

The Barber Shop and Antique
Mall buildings look the same
on the outside, but they have
different names and owners
and my legs don't feel steady
enough to venture inside
to check out new antiques.

We park right up to the door
of the Good Apple and arm
in arm, my husband and I waltz
through the door and find
nothing has changed except
for the clerks and prices
since we first started shopping
in the store in 2000.

We walk down the aisle
past the bins of bulk
rice, cinnamon and flour
to the organic produce section
where we buy strawberries
and watermelon, to the coolers
where we pick up Flaxseed Oil
to the shelves where we buy
Lutein. Calcium and Vitamin B
and as we go out the door
we pick up cones swirled
with frozen yogurt. Black cherry
for me, chocolate for him,
like we have for two decades
and lick them in the air conditioned
car before driving home in 110 degrees.

Second Outing Since the Fall

Spine straight as an Oak tree,
I grip the handlebars of the shopping cart
and push it across the parking lot
and through the sliding glass doors
past the pumpkins, masks and costumes
to the clothes clearance racks
expecting to dodge carts veering
in my lane, sideswiping or tailgating.

But all I see is a white haired woman
with a camel's hump pushing a cart
and a young Hispanic man pressing
his cell phone to the same shorts
I am eying while his wife shouts:
What is the size? on the other end.

I see three empty hangers
and a pile of red shorts
lying limp as linguini on the floor
I want to bend over and pick
them up and put them
on their hangers like I used
to do but I know I will lose
my balance and join them.

By the time I pick out two pairs
of pants my size, I spot my husband,
walking down the aisle, his cart
packed with produce, poultry and pop.

In the intersection, I hand him my
clothes and he moves on to check-out.

Pushing the cart holding my purse
and a water bottle, I head for the exit
where a white-haired woman checks receipts.
I tell her my sad story to explain
why I have a water bottle I brought
in the store and no receipt
and tell her I need to sit on a bench
inside the door. *Are you okay?* She asks
as I attempt to quiet my shaking limbs.

Having figured out I am not a shoplifter,
and there is no need to call security,
she waves me through but keeps asking:
Are you okay? as customers show receipts
and I sit on the bench until my husband arrives
and I realize I have survived my first
walk through Wal-Mart after the fall.

Dear Loretta

I was never a Coal Miners Daughter
from Butchers Hollow, never got
pregnant in my teens and never could
carry a tune but I worshipped you
when bare foot and pregnant you took the stage
in the sixties and shocked the country
singing songs you penned about birth control,
and fist fighting with floozies
who were sleeping with your husband
while birthing and bathing six babies.
I cheered when you humbly accepted eight
Country Music Awards including the first
female Country Entertainer of the Year
half a century ago. I worried when you
suffered a stroke and then fractured
your hip after falling off the stage
in your mid-eighties. I cried when barely
two weeks after you warbled
your last note at the age of ninety,
your successors, sixty something
redheaded Reba and thirty-nine-year-old
blondes Carrie and Miranda
sang your songs at the CMA Awards,
hoping your spirit would make one
of the blondes the first CMA female
entertainer of the year in ten years
and only the eighth in fifty-nine years.
Since they lost to a male, be an angel
and finish your work, Loretta.

Acceptance

It's the Husband

the detective on Dateline
says as he bends over
the cold body of the wife.
He had murder on his mind,
says his partner, picking
up the bloody butcher knife.
*And he cleaned the crime
scene*, he says smelling bleach
on the wet rags in the sink.

If those two detectives
came to my house,
they'd find my husband
cleaning the kitchen
with dinner on his mind
and my warm body in bed.
They'd find the butcher
knife slick with slices
of watermelon he slides
on a plate for a snack.

Do you want fish or chicken?
Salad or soup? he asks
as he relaxes in the recliner
and spears his watermelon
with a fork. The detectives
would find this an act
of aggression and cuff
him and place him in the back
of the police car as his hearing
aides squeal as loud as the sirens.

Who's the Stranger in My House?

Grumpy and grumbling
he gathers up the empty
smoothie cup and breakfast
dishes. Wild white weeds
the color of his hair sprout
on his face. A bramble bush
turns into a tumbleweed.

In the photos on the wall,
he is Al Pacino, a gangster
in The Godfather. Sleek
short dark hair, bushy brows,
clean shaven, standing next
to me blonde as Beverly D'Angelo.
But the stranger sleeping in my bed
looks more like Grizzly Adams.

Why are you growing a beard?
I ask. *No time to shave*, he answers
sweat soaking his shirt from the sun
shining on solar panels he installs
on the roof, after sitting in darkness
as thunder blasts and lightning
flashes like gunfire in a muzzle.

One day I find an empty box
of Just for Men black hair color
in the bathroom waste basket
and Pacino, short dark hair and clean

shaven, reappears, impersonating
Jimmy Hoffa in The Irishman:
I may have my faults, but being wrong
ain't one of them, as light floods the room
and a gangster replaces a grizzly.

Handy to be Married to a Handy Man

The Arizona Monsoons knock out
the power so he fires up the generator
as he has for twenty years but it conks
out as we play Gin Rummy. Twenty minutes
later, he appears in the lighted doorway
announcing that the power is back on.

Does that mean we need a new generator?
I ask. *I fixed it farmer style,* he says. *Give me
duct tape, chewing gum and bailing wire
and I can repair anything. Didn't you watch
MacGyver?* Yes, but I also watched him.

He lies under the sink holding a pipe
spewing water out of many holes. *Bring me
super glue and plastic wraps,* he says.
and I fetch them like a floppy eared
spaniel bringing a ball on the beach.

The Cadillac lurches to a stop on a dirt road
in the middle of the steaming Arizona desert.
He crawls under the car. Our grandson
sticks his head in the window. *Hand me
your fingernail polish and rubber bands,*
he says to his older and younger sisters.

They shake their heads, ponytails bobbing.
but relent when he says. *It's burgers and fries
or you walk home.* The car starts and in seconds
we are in Sonic, the sisters' hair flowing as fast
as the mustard, ketchup and cokes over ice.

Why I Never Learn to Swim

Did you drown? The swimming instructor
asks me when I panic as I float on my belly
and she is no longer holding me up. I thrash
around like a trout on a fishing line.

If I drowned, I'd be dead, I laugh. I recall
at eight being pushed in the pool and hitting
my head and watching a child with my same
swimsuit lying on the bottom in the deep end.

The next thing I know I feel a whoosh
and I am back in my body outside of the water
and I wake up spurting water like a whale
while a teenage lifeguard straddles me.

Now I am eighteen working on a Wyoming
ranch, I want to learn to swim so I can
go out on a boat and swim with the dudes.
Before my next lesson, I get the chance.

I throw off my life jacket and jump
in the Snake River remembering
the swim teacher's instructions:
Just float and the water will hold you up.

But she lied because the water sweeps
and swirls and I'm whirling in a washing
machine that won't stop. One second
I see shore and the next blue water.

I kick my feet and thrash my arms
and I sink as water swishes and fills
my eyes, nose and mouth until I stop
struggling and my mind goes blank.

I float over shore where a teenage
girl I recognize as me sprawls in the sand.
A crowd gathers and the dude ranch
foreman gives her CPR like on TV.

I lose interest as I lie on soft clouds
among the saffron yellow and magenta colors
and then I feel a tug on my suit and I am
pulled back into my body where I sit up.
You're fine, the foreman says.
You got caught up in a whirlpool.
But as I rest, he whispers voice shaking:
She was dead for a good five minutes.

The Tale of the Dying Refrigerator

Pale and dried up, the twenty
year old Kenmore,
with a life expectancy
of fifteen years,
wheezes and whines
in our Arizona desert kitchen
like a patient in ICU.

Forty miles away in Mesa,
shiny and brand new
like a newborn in the nursery,
the silver Samsung spits out
chunky cubes of ice
and ejects streams of water.

I'll take it, my husband says
and hands the salesman
his credit card. *It will be delivered
in four days*, the salesman says,
squinting at the computer screen,
and hands him the receipt.

We have to reschedule.
We don't deliver in your area
until Thursday, the young woman
with the whiney voice says.
We'll email on Wednesday night
and delivery will call Thursday
thirty minutes before they show up.

The old refrigerator shivers
and shakes, teeth chattering.

They rerouted us to the wrong
area. We'll deliver next Thursday,
the deliveryman says into the phone.
Hang on. I whisper and hug
the big box but all I hear
is a beeping sound like hospital
life support machines.

Three Thursdays later, a truck
backs up to the kitchen door
and two burly guys wheel
in the shiny silver Samsung.
We pull the plug and the Kenmore.
dies. The Samsung hums a melody
as perfectly formed ice cubes
fall into the cup followed
by a stream of cold water.
This baby is a keeper.

Tis the Season

Going outside. Got to get the roof fixed
before the monsoons, my husband says
as I sit at the computer answering emails.
I feel something soft moving
under my bare feet and scramble
on unsteady legs, knee screaming.

A two-inch creature crawls towards me.
as I squint through eighty-year-old eyes.
Is it a tarantula, scorpion, or another
desert creature escaping the hot sun?

The saw screeches from the sun porch.
I stare out the sliding glass door
as my husband climbs the ladder to the roof.
The creature follows me as hanging
onto the bedpost I head for the shoe
pile next to the nightstand so I can
walk outside and call to him.

As I pick up the only shoe that fits
my swollen foot, I turn and a tiny mouse
stares up at me. My heart lurches
and I drop the shoe. *Where's your mother?*
I ask the trembling creature at my feet.

I find a cup on the nightstand
and place it in front of the mouse
which freezes and stands and stares.

I shut the door and collapse on the couch
until my husband appears. *Are you okay?*

There's a baby mouse in the bedroom, I say.
We've got to find the mother. My husband
opens the door, scoots the mouse into the cup
and as he heads out, says. *I just released*
a big mouse outside this morning.

Two frogs hop down the hallway
and a lizard perched on the couch watches
as the baby mouse runs to his mother.
Tis the summer season, I say, laughing.

Mr. Crow

Short, squat and solid,
a businessman in black,
he struts across our property
like he just bought it,

to the waterfalls
to dunk the bagel
or bangles he stole
from the table, floor
or dumpster
at the sidewalk café.

Then he inspects
the seeds – sunflower,
pumpkin, watermelon,
cantaloupe - we discard
and buries them
in the fertile soil.

Some sprout into green
vines and plants
that survive until the cows
or wildlife eat them
long after Mr. Crow
flies away to never return.

Cactus Wren

The brown backed
white bellied bird
chirps like the smoke
detector as flames
dance in the fireplace,

frantically flying back
and forth from the counters
to the cabinets to the windowsills.
Most likely a sister or brother
of the cholla dweller who
tours the kitchen two weeks
ago as my husband hauls
in groceries from the Cadillac.

Could be a cousin to the cactus wren
we find perched on the ice cream cone
cookie jar in the dining room a decade ago.
Or an ancestor of Charley who scolds my husband
for building a house in his habitat two decades ago.

The current visitor swoops over my head
and disappears into the dark living room.
We go about our business until we hear
a screeching SOS call and the flapping of wings
and open the door and the bird follows the light
and disappears down the dirt driveway.

We breathe a sigh of relief until five days
later, I hear chirping again and find another
cactus wren flying through the house
and then every morning we find another
and another. Then a missing vent
on the side of the house gives away
that they are nesting in the attic
and hopping down into the house
like tenants exploring hidden rooms.

Ultimate Feast

At Red Lobster in Pocatello,
I order the Ultimate Feast:
lobster tail, crab legs, shrimp
scampi and shrimp on a stick
with a green salad and cheddar biscuits
on our first anniversary for $26.89.

At Red Lobster in Salt Lake
and Mesa, I order the same
Ultimate Feast for birthdays
and anniversaries for years
sharing it with family and friends,
until the price reaches $36.89
and we stop eating in restaurants.

For our 26th anniversary, I check
out Red Lobster's menu and find:
Ultimate Family Feast for $122.89.
Maine lobster tails, wild-caught
North American snow crab legs,
garlic shrimp scampi
and Walt's Favorite Shrimp.
Served with two family-style
sides and eight cheddar biscuits.

Since it's only us, we dine on corn
on the cob, salad with prawns
and whole wheat bread at sunset.
The sky streaks scarlet as a buck,

doe and fawn creep past the Cholla,
Mesquite and Palo Verde, and stop
as they see us sitting at the picnic table.
Forks freeze in the mountain air
and they walk over and drink the cool
well water out of our waterfalls/pond,
providing us with the ultimate feast.

Margaret and Me

We are our grandmothers
standing outside a closed door
waiting for our voices to be heard

in the poetry reading hall. We hear
voices inside and jiggle the knob
and pound on the locked door.

Her white hair fluffs around her face.
One knee swollen like a shitake
throbs as she leans on a cane.

My shoulders shrink under the sheet
of white hair hanging to my waist
as my feet flame like fire on the walker.

*You are discriminating against old
ladies and daughters of immigrants*, I shout.
The door squeaks open and we file in.

Tap tap tap, we shuffle to the podium,
our words wailing off the walls
and hands clapping like the waves

that washed the ships up on the shore
carrying our ancestors from foreign lands
so we can be free to speak our truth.

Saying Goodbye to Bobby

Vultures feast on a coyote
carcass as we caravan
along the Superstition Highway
from Queen Valley to Superior
like we did for decades
with Bobby, the leader
of the band, to eat
Chimichangas and bean
burritos at Los Hermanos
and drink beer and play gigs
at Porters, Bobby's growly deep voice
booming louder than a microphone
when he sang *Sixteen Tons* and *Lodi*
for six decades, now silenced.

Those of us who outlive our legend
inhale the crisp mountain air
as we stop along the side of the road
and climb the hill to the top of the tunnel
between Superior and Globe to honor
his last wishes. I see Bobby floating
in a cloud canoe in the blue sea sky on Top
Of the World in his woolen long Johns,
his mouth making music as he strums
an acoustic guitar. Wanda with wings
flies beside him playing the bass
with Gene in his goatee playing the dobro
as he floats on his back next to Bobby.

As Bobby's blue eyes peer over his bushy
beard, his straw cowboy hat he had worn
at every gig is whipped by the wind
and boomerangs down the cavern
followed by his ashes swirling like smoke.
And we look up into the sky and Bobby is gone.

Reading Obits of Past Bosses and Boyfriends

He passed away at his home at 97
surrounded by his loving family.
He was caring, loving and generous.
In the sixties, my boss frowns and frets
because his steak is too rare, pecks
the cheek of his pear-shaped wife
as she flies off back east never to return
leaving him with a tantrum throwing
two-year-old sitting in his limousine
as he stashes cash in overseas accounts.

It is with heavy hearts we announce
the death of our beloved brother and son
who joined his savior at sixty-two.
While he lives a block from the store
where his mother, brother and sister
sell carpet and furniture, they haven't
spoken for a decade and decline
to be a part of his intervention
even though I tell them about his liver
pain when he turns forty. *He'll be fine,*
they say as a customer comes in.

Helen went to her home in Heaven
at the age of eighty-seven.
She was an angel always sacrificing
herself for others. Helen's nine-year-old
daughter sobs when she forces her

to live with her father. *I want to live
alone,* Helen says. *My teenagers
live on the streets because their father
and stepfather didn't want them,*
she says as she smiles. On her desk
sits a vase of roses a client sends me after
I hold her hand as we wait for the ambulance
when she falls on the ice on the sidewalk
while Helen watches through glass.
I must have an admirer, Helen says.

I remember the sixties when I wrote
obits, only sticking to the facts, no
lies and no family interference. Now
I write my own obit stating I died
leaving my family to fill in the blanks -
how, where, when or at what age -
and like a painter airbrush my past
so it highlights my accomplishments
and erases my mistakes.

Made in the USA
Middletown, DE
30 January 2023

22158416R00052